The Lasso Guide:
100+ Motivational Quotes

The Lasso Guide:
100+ Motivational Quotes

The Lasso Guide: 100+ MotivationallQuotes
© 2024 Independently published by Blue Press
United States
This publication has not been prepared, approved, licensed, or authorized by the creators or
producers of Ted Lasso or any entity involved in creating or producing the well-known Apple+ TV
show Ted Lasso.

Cover design by: Blue Press
Printed in the United States of America
All rights reserved.

INTRODUCTION

Welcome to the world of Ted Lasso where optimism reigns supreme, and every challenge is an opportunity for growth. "The Ted Lasso Guide: 100+ Motivational Ted Lasso Quotes" is a collection that brings to life the heartwarming and motivational wisdom of the beloved hit TV show. In a world often dominated by cynicism and doubt, Ted Lasso stands as a beacon of hope, reminding us of the incredible power of a positive outlook and unwavering determination.

Through the pages of this book, you'll find a treasure trove of quotes that encapsulate the essence of "Ted Lasso." These words are more than just lines from a script; they are pearls of wisdom that have resonated with audiences worldwide. Whether you're a fan of the show or simply seeking a dose of encouragement, these quotes will uplift your spirit, spark your motivation, and guide you toward a brighter perspective on life's challenges.

Ted Lasso is more than a character; he's an embodiment of the values that make us better people: kindness, empathy, and the belief that everyone has the potential to shine. From the ever-optimistic Ted Lasso himself to the diverse cast of characters that surround him, the show reminds us that embracing positivity isn't about ignoring difficulties—it's about facing them head-on with a smile and a willingness to learn.

As you delve into the pages of this book, let these quotes serve as a source of inspiration on your journey. Whether you're navigating a rough patch or striving for personal and professional success, the words of Ted Lasso and his team will offer guidance and comfort. These quotes are a reminder that even in the face of adversity, you have the power to create your own destiny, and with the right attitude, you can turn challenges into stepping stones toward greatness.

So, let the journey begin. May these quotes uplift your spirits, ignite your passions, and encourage you to approach life with open arms and an unwavering belief in the goodness that surrounds us. Let's take a page from Ted Lasso's playbook and remember that, in the end, it's not just about winning—it's about the journey, the relationships, and the impact we make along the way.

"You know what the happiest animal on Earth is? It's a goldfish. You know why? Got a 10-second memory. Be a goldfish, Sam."

"It's like a good buddy of mine used to say, 'There's two buttons I never like to hit: panic and snooze.'"

"Do you believe in ghosts? I do. I do believe in ghosts. Not the sort of ghosts that float through walls, but the ones that haunt us. Who we were, who we are, who we can't be anymore."

"You're off to a fresh start, and just remember, be curious, not judgmental."

"Taking on a challenge is a lot like riding a horse. If you're comfortable while you're doing it, you're probably doing it wrong."

"Success is not about the destination, it's about the journey."

"I believe in hope. I believe in believe. I believe in being a goldfish."

"You don't want to win the same way all the time. That's boring. And winning, it ain't about playing perfect. It's about how you respond to your mistakes."

"The first step in avoiding judgment is, to be honest with yourself."

"You have no idea how many times I've heard that I'm crazy, or that I'm making a mistake, or that I'm just flat out doing the wrong thing. And every time, it only made me stronger."

"Be curious, not judgmental."

"As the man once said, the harder you work, the luckier you get."

"If the internet has taught us anything,
it's that sometimes it's easier to speak
our minds anonymously."

"You've gotta be comfortable being uncomfortable."

"Anger is like swallowing poison and expecting the other person to die."

"You can't force a flower to bloom, but you can water it."

**"It's okay to be sad, but it's not okay
to do nothing."**

"The longer you wait for something, the more you'll appreciate it when you get it, because anything worth having is definitely worth waiting for."

"I don't think we can start over. I think we just need to move forward."

"The world is full of people ready to call you a failure. Don't give them the satisfaction."

"You know, sometimes the best way to get through stuff is to hold onto each other."

"You see, when it comes to belief, you don't have to have the same opinion as others. But if you start from a place of respect, humility, and an acknowledgment of their experiences, well, then, that's your first step to building a bridge."

"The best way to get something done
is to begin."

"Every day is a chance to be better, to be the best version of yourself."

"It's hard to be cynical. It's harder than being optimistic."

"I think we're all faced with moments where we can do better. And it's those moments that become the stories that define us."

"We're gonna lose games, and you're gonna be a part of it. But at the end of the day, it's about how you carry yourself."

"It's the not knowing that makes it exciting, right? The future is a big, beautiful question mark."

"When it comes to your own problems, sometimes it's best to not look at the bigger picture."

"It's not about whether you win or lose, it's about how you play the game."

"It's never a sign of weakness to ask
for help when you need it."

"The longer you stew in indecision, the harder it is to remember the right answer."

"You know what? We can either continue to hurt each other, or we can choose forgiveness."

"We've all got a bit of darkness in us. Sometimes we need someone to help us turn on the lights."

"You have to take ownership of the mistakes, but you cannot wallow in them."

"It's never too late to be who you might have been."

"All I want is for you to be the best version of yourself."

"It's easy to be brave from a safe distance away."

"If you look at it just right, you'll find that hope is kind of like dominos. Once one falls, the rest follow."

"I don't know everything, but I do know that you've got to care about people more than wins and losses."

"You know, sometimes the happiest people are the ones who don't fit neatly into boxes."

"The truth is, no matter how you ended up at this juncture, you're here now. And that's what I'm excited about."

"Kindness is free, but it's also priceless."

"The future is still completely unspoiled."

"You know, the hard thing is the right thing."

"Life is short, and it's better when you're laughing."

"You don't win games with your fists. You win games with your feet, and your heart, and your mind."

"It's the little things that make up the big things."

"Sometimes the best advice is just to be yourself."

"You know, it's like those older folks say, 'The happiest people are the givers, not the getters.'"

"You know, sometimes your joy is the source of your smile, but sometimes your smile can be the source of your joy."

"You know what's the worst thing? You don't even know what you don't know."

"You have to be a good teammate
before you can be a good team."

"The past is written, but the future is up for grabs."

"You know what's the most important thing in life? Gratitude."

"Just remember, be curious, not judgmental."

"Change is never easy, but it's always worth it."

**"Sometimes the best thing you can do
is just be there for someone."**

"You can't control the outcome, but you can control your effort."

"You know, it's not the size of the dog in the fight, it's the size of the fight in the dog."

"You don't have to be alone in your struggles."

"You don't have to be perfect to be valuable."

"You have to find joy in the process, not just the outcome."

*"Forgiveness doesn't mean forgetting,
it means letting go of the hurt."*

"Every day is a new opportunity to learn and grow."

"You know, life is funny. And sometimes it's not even that. It's just life."

"You can either let adversity define you, or you can let it refine you."

"It's the simplest gestures that make us feel valued and seen."

"It's not about being the best. It's about being better than you were yesterday."

"It's okay to be scared. Being scared means you're about to do something really, really brave."

"You ever heard the expression 'You catch more flies with honey than you do with vinegar?'"

"You don't have to be the best at something to be worth something."

"Football is a simple game. And sometimes the simplest move is the most effective one."

"Every day means every day."

"If you care about someone, and you got a little love in your heart, there ain't nothing you can't get through together."

"I think things come into our lives to help us get from one place to a better one."

"Just listen to your gut, and on the way down to your gut, check in with your heart. Between those two things, they'll let you know what's what."

"I believe in Communism. Rom-communism, that is. If Tom Hanks and Meg Ryan can go through some heartfelt struggles and still end up happy, then so can we."

"Doing the right thing is never the wrong thing."

"You know how they say that 'youth is wasted on the young'? Well, I say don't let the wisdom of age be wasted on you."

"It may not work out how you think it will or how you hope it does. But believe me, it will all work out."

"You beating yourself up is like Woody Allen playing the clarinet. I don't wanna hear it."

"Best teachers are the toughest ones."

"You say impossible, but all I hear is 'I'm possible.'"

*"Living in the moment, it's a gift.
That's why they call it the present."*

"What do you say we do what the man says and make today our masterpiece?"

"The truth will set you free, but first it will piss you off."

"Your body is like day-old rice. If it ain't warmed up properly, something real bad could happen."

"I lost my way for a minute, but I'm on the road back."

"Every disadvantage has its advantage."

"I shouldn't bring an umbrella to a brainstorm."

"I suppose the best brand is being yourself."

"Smells like potential."

"Old people are so wise. They're like tall Yodas."

"Isn't the idea of 'never give up' one of them things we always talk about in sports? And shouldn't that apply to people too?"

"Coach, I'm me. Why would I want to be anything else?"

"I like the idea of someone becoming rich because of what they gave to the world, not just because of who their family is."

"I want you to know, I value each of your opinions, even when you're wrong."

"Our goal is to go out like Willie Nelson — on a high!"

"Most of the time change is a good thing and I think that's what it's all about—embracing change, being brave, doing whatever you have to so everyone in your life can move forward with theirs."

"For me, success is not about the wins and losses. It's about helping these young fellas be the best versions of themselves on and off the field."

"Sometimes a smile is the best way to spread sunshine."

"The best way to cope with a difficult situation is to turn it into an opportunity."

"I'll tell you what I'm going to do: I'm going to believe in myself."

"It's never too late to start all over again."

"The diamond formation: hard and focused, tough to crack, yet with enough rough edges to shine. Now, let's be diamonds."

"Believe."

Printed in Great Britain
by Amazon

41620934R00064